A COMPENDIUM OF KNOWLEDGE

THE ENLIGHTENED MIND

TAJ PIERRE

VOIR DIRE PUBLISHING

THE ENLIGHTENED MIND

A COMPENDIUM OF KNOWLEDGE

―――

TAJ PIERRE

All Rights Reserved

Copyright © 2024 Voir Dire Publishing

No part of this publication may be reproduced, distributed, or transmitted in any form or by any means, including photocopying, recording, or other electronic or mechanical methods, without the prior written permission of the publisher, except in the case of brief quotations embodied in critical reviews and certain other noncommercial uses permitted by copyright law.

For permission requests, write to the publisher at the address below:

Voir Dire Publishing

5350 Bellaire Blvd. #3356

Bellaire, TX 77402

ISBN: 979-8-9891756-1-1

Printed in the United States of America

TABLE OF CONTENTS

Chapter 1 - The Foundations of Human Thought..................1

Chapter 2 - Introduction to Philosophy and Life's Big Questions 7

Chapter 3 - Mathematics: The Language of the Universe......12

Chapter 4 - History: Lessons from the past....................19

Chapter 5 - Literature: Windows into Other Worlds...................27

Chapter 6 - Art and Creativity: Expressing the Inexpressible.....32

Chapter 7 - Psychology: Unlocking the Human Mind................39

Chapter 8 - Technology: Tools for Tomorrow................45

Chapter 9 - Economics: The Science of Scarcity and Choice..................51

Chapter 10 - Politics and Governance: Power in Practice.....59

Chapter 11 - Ethics and Morality: The Compass for Action...64

Chapter 12 - Environmental Studies: The Planet We Call Home..................70

Chapter 13 - Social Justice: Fostering Equality and Fairness.....77

Chapter 14 - Health and Wellness: The Body and Mind Connection..................83

Chapter 15 - Communication: Bridging Minds and Ideas..... 89

Chapter 16 - World Religions: Diverse Paths to Meaning 95

Chapter 17 - Emotional Intelligence: The Other Side of Smart 100

Chapter 18 - Gender Studies: Beyond Binary Perspectives 104

Chapter 19 - Education: The Lifelong Journey 108

Chapter 20 - Relationships: The Ties that Bind 113

Chapter 21 - Time Management: Making Every Moment Count 118

Chapter 22 - The Pursuit of Happiness: An Eternal Quest 123

Chapter 23 - Digital Dynamics and Cyber Fortress: Mastering the Art of Security in the Digital Revolution Era 131

Chapter 24 - Navigating the Digital Maze: Thriving in the Age of Information Overload 137

Chapter 25 - Cosmic Frontiers: Voyages Beyond Earth's Bounds 142

Composers Final Thoughts 147

CHAPTER 1
THE FOUNDATIONS OF HUMAN THOUGHT

Human thought, the elusive yet omnipresent phenomenon, shapes civilizations, technologies, and indeed the very fabric of human society. What makes human cognition so unique? What are its evolutionary roots? How are different components like language, culture, and technology interlinked with human thought? This chapter delves into the intricate landscape that comprises the foundations of human thought.

Cognitive Evolution

Cognitive evolution refers to the process through which the cognitive abilities of organisms, particularly humans, have developed over time through biological evolution. This process involves changes in the brain and its functioning, leading to advanced mental capacities. Understanding cognitive evolution is crucial for comprehending how humans have come to possess unique mental abilities.

Early Stages of Cognitive Evolution

The earliest stages of cognitive evolution are seen in the most primitive organisms. Simple life forms exhibit basic cognitive functions such as response to stimuli and basic learning. As evolution progressed, these basic functions became more complex. For instance, invertebrates like cephalopods display remarkable problem-solving skills, indicating an early form of complex cognition.

The Role of Primates in Cognitive Evolution

Primates, especially the great apes, have played a significant role in cognitive evolution. The development of larger brain sizes in primates correlates with more complex behaviors and social structures. For example, chimpanzees use tools and have intricate social hierarchies, illustrating advanced cognitive abilities compared to other animals.

Human Cognitive Evolution

Humans represent the pinnacle of cognitive evolution. The human brain, particularly the neocortex, is much larger relative to body size than in any other species. This enlargement has enabled advanced cognitive functions such as language, abstract thinking, and problem-solving.

1. Language and Communication: Language is a critical aspect of human cognitive evolution. It has enabled complex communication, the transmission of culture, and the sharing of ideas, contributing to societal development.
2. Abstract Thinking and Problem Solving: Humans excel in abstract thinking – the ability to understand concepts that are not grounded in physical experience. This ability is crucial for mathematics, science, and philosophy.
3. Social Cognition: Human evolution has been significantly influenced by social interactions. The ability to understand others' intentions and

emotions (theory of mind) has been vital for cooperation and social cohesion.

Neurological Developments

The evolution of the brain is a key aspect of cognitive evolution. The development of certain brain areas has been critical:

- Prefrontal Cortex: Responsible for decision making, planning, and social behavior.
- Temporal Lobes: Involved in memory and language processing.
- Parietal Lobes: Important for spatial orientation and manipulation.

Impact of Environmental Changes

Environmental changes have been a driving force in cognitive evolution. For example, the shift from forested areas to savannahs in Africa likely played a role in the development of bipedalism and subsequently in cognitive changes in early humans.

Tool Use and Technology

Tool use has been a significant factor in cognitive evolution. The development and use of tools require understanding cause and effect, problem-solving, and planning.

Cultural Evolution and Cognitive Development

Cultural evolution has also impacted cognitive development. The accumulation and transmission of cultural knowledge have allowed humans to build upon the discoveries of previous generations, leading to exponential growth in knowledge and technology.

Genetics and Cognitive Evolution

Genetic mutations and natural selection have driven cognitive evolution. Certain genetic changes, particularly in genes related to brain development, have had profound impacts on cognitive abilities.

Challenges and Critiques

There are challenges in studying cognitive evolution, including the lack of direct evidence from the fossil record about cognitive abilities. Critics argue that cognitive abilities cannot be directly inferred from brain size or structure alone.

The Future of Cognitive Evolution

The future of cognitive evolution may be influenced by technology, such as artificial intelligence and genetic engineering, potentially leading to new forms of cognition.

Primate Beginnings

The emergence of complex cognitive abilities can be traced back to our primate ancestors. Basic cognitive functions like problem-solving, social learning, and the use of tools were first observed in primates, setting the stage for more advanced cognitive development.

Homo Sapiens: A Cognitive Leap

Modern humans display a remarkable leap in cognitive capabilities. The emergence of abstract reasoning, planning, and language have been attributed to the development of the prefrontal cortex, a region of the brain involved in executive functions.

CHAPTER 2
INTRODUCTION TO PHILOSOPHY AND LIFE'S BIG QUESTIONS

Philosophy, at its core, is the love of wisdom. It's a pursuit that has driven humans to ask profound questions about their existence, the universe, and the principles governing both. The questions that philosophy tackles are as vast as they are deep: What is the meaning of life? Is there a right way to live? What is reality? Such inquiries not only offer intellectual stimulation but also guide us in navigating the complexities of life.

The Meaning of Life: A Perennial Question

One of the most enduring questions in philosophy is about the meaning of life. Throughout history, various schools of thought have proposed different answers. The ancient Greeks, like Aristotle, believed in eudaemonia, a form of flourishing achieved through virtuous living. In contrast, existentialists like Jean-Paul Sartre posited that life has no inherent meaning, and it's up to each individual to create their own.

Ethics and Morality: The Guideposts of Conduct

Philosophy also delves into the realm of ethics and morality, exploring questions about right and wrong. Ethical theories, ranging from utilitarianism, which advocates for the greatest good for the greatest number, to Kantian ethics, which emphasizes duty and intention, offer diverse perspectives on how to live a moral life. These theories are not just academic; they influence real-world decisions and policies.

The Nature of Reality: Understanding Our Existence

Another fundamental philosophical query is about the nature of reality. Philosophers like Plato and Descartes pondered what's truly real versus what's perceived. In contemporary times, discussions about simulation theory and the advent of virtual reality technology bring new dimensions to these ancient debates.

The Pursuit of Happiness: A Philosophical Journey

Happiness is a goal that most people strive for, but what is it exactly, and how do we achieve it? Philosophers have offered varying views on this. The Stoics, for example, advocated for a life of virtue in accordance with nature as the path to true happiness, while Epicureans emphasized the pursuit of pleasure and the avoidance of pain.

Free Will and Determinism: The Control Over Our Fate

The debate between free will and determinism questions the extent of human agency. Do we genuinely have free will, or are our choices predetermined by factors beyond our control? This question has implications for everything from personal responsibility to legal systems.

The Role of Knowledge: Understanding Versus Believing

Epistemology, the study of knowledge, asks how we know what we know. It challenges the distinction between belief and true knowledge. Philosophers like John Locke and Immanuel Kant have contributed significantly to this field, offering insights into the nature and limits of human understanding.

The Search for Truth: A Philosophical Odyssey

The quest for truth is a central theme in philosophy. Philosophers employ logic and reasoning to uncover truths about the world and our place in it. This pursuit is not only about finding answers but also about asking better questions.

The Intersection of Science and Philosophy

In recent times, the relationship between philosophy and science has become increasingly important. Philosophers like Karl Popper and Thomas Kuhn have explored the nature of scientific inquiry and progress, shedding light on how we understand scientific truths.

Philosophy teaches us that while definitive answers to life's big questions may be elusive, there is profound value in the quest itself. The journey through philosophical inquiry not only enriches our understanding of the world but also shapes how we live our lives. As we navigate life's complexities, philosophy remains a guiding light, illuminating paths through the fog of existence.

This chapter provides a brief exploration into some of the fundamental questions of philosophy. Each section can be expanded upon with more detailed examples, historical context, and contemporary applications

CHAPTER 3
MATHEMATICS: THE LANGUAGE OF THE UNIVERSE

This language is often seen as the underlying code or syntax through which the cosmos communicates its principles, patterns, and mysteries. Let's delve into this intriguing subject in an in-depth manner.

Mathematics: The Universal Syntax

Mathematics is frequently hailed as the language of the universe. This idea stems from the observation that mathematical principles underpin the physical laws governing everything from the microscopic world of quantum mechanics to the vast expanse of cosmology.

The Elegance of Numbers and Equations

Mathematics' ability to describe and predict natural phenomena with precision is one of its most remarkable features. The elegance of equations, like Einstein's famous $E=mc^2$, speaks to a deep harmony between mathematical abstraction and physical reality. This alignment suggests that the universe operates according to mathematical principles, whether we're looking at the orbit of planets, the patterns in a sunflower, or the structure of a snowflake.

Geometry: The Shape of Reality

Geometry, especially, has a special place in deciphering the language of the universe. The geometric shapes and patterns – think of the Fibonacci sequence appearing in spiral galaxies and nautilus shells – illustrate how geometry is a foundational syntax of the natural world.

Physics: Deciphering the Cosmic Code

Physics takes the mathematical language and applies it to understand the laws that govern matter, energy, space, and time.

Quantum Mechanics: The Subatomic Dialect

Quantum mechanics, with its probability waves and uncertainty principles, reveals a universe that speaks in probabilities and possibilities. This quantum "dialect" is fundamentally different from the deterministic language of classical physics, presenting a more nuanced and complex syntax.

Relativity: The Grammar of Space and Time

Einstein's theory of relativity introduced a new grammar in the language of the universe, where space and time are interwoven into a single continuum. This has radically changed our understanding of the universe, introducing concepts like time dilation and space-time curvature.

Cosmology: The Storytelling of the Universe

Cosmology is the study of the universe as a whole, from its inception to its ultimate fate. It's like reading the universe's autobiography.

The Big Bang and Cosmic Evolution

The Big Bang theory, which describes the universe's birth and subsequent expansion, is a narrative written in the language of cosmological physics. It tells a story of a universe evolving over billions of years, from a singularity to the vast cosmos we observe today.

Dark Matter and Dark Energy: The Unknown Characters

Despite our growing understanding, there are 'words' in the universe's language that we have yet to understand fully. Concepts like dark matter and dark energy remind us that there are aspects of the universal language that remain mysterious and elusive.

Philosophy and Spirituality: Interpreting the Cosmic Dialogue

In philosophy and spirituality, the language of the universe often takes on more abstract and metaphysical meanings.

The Universe as a Conscious Entity

Some philosophical and spiritual traditions interpret the universe as a conscious, intelligent entity. In this view, the language of the universe is one of consciousness, where physical reality is just one expression of a deeper, spiritual essence.

Patterns and Synchronicities

Patterns, synchronicities, and the concept of "As above, so below" in hermetic philosophies suggest that there is a correspondence between the various planes of existence. This implies a language that transcends just physical laws, encompassing a more holistic, universal principle.

The Language of the Universe in Art and Culture

Art and culture often reflect humanity's attempt to articulate and engage with the universe's language.

Artistic Representations

Artists across time have tried to capture the essence of the universe's language through paintings, music, literature, and sculpture. These works often reflect the human awe and wonder at the cosmos's complexity and beauty.

Mythology and Storytelling

Myths and stories from various cultures can be seen as metaphorical interpretations of the universe's language. They often personify natural forces and cosmic events, giving them a narrative that can be more easily understood and related to.

The Unending Quest to Understand

The quest to fully understand the language of the universe is ongoing. It spans across disciplines, cultures, and philosophies. This language is not static; it evolves as our understanding deepens and our perspective widens. The exploration of this language is not just a scientific or intellectual pursuit; it's a journey that touches on the very essence of what it means to be human and our place in the cosmos.

A dialect spoken in the patterns of galaxies, the dance of subatomic particles, and the philosophical musings of human minds. As we continue to study and interpret this language, we not only uncover the secrets of the cosmos but also understand ourselves.

CHAPTER 4
HISTORY: LESSONS FROM THE PAST

The study of history is not just a mere recollection of dates and events but a treasure trove of lessons and insights. With a vicariously prudent examination of the past, we gain a clearer understanding of our present and can better navigate our future. This chapter explores various historical periods and themes, gleaning unique lessons from each.

Lessons from Ancient Civilizations

Ancient civilizations, such as those of Egypt, Greece, and Mesopotamia, offer profound lessons in governance, philosophy, and the human spirit. The Egyptian civilization, for example, teaches us the importance of architectural innovation and the value of a well-organized societal structure. Greek civilization, known for its philosophers like Socrates, Plato, and Aristotle, highlights the significance of questioning and reasoning in human development. Mesopotamia, often regarded as the cradle of civilization, provides insights into the development of writing systems and law.

Medieval Times: A Lesson in Resilience and Transition

The medieval period, often misunderstood as an age of darkness, was actually a time of significant transformation. This era saw the rise of feudalism, the spread of religions, and the beginning of the Renaissance. The resilience of human societies in the face of challenges like the Black Death and the Hundred Years' War teaches us about the enduring spirit of humanity and the inevitable nature of change.

The Renaissance: Humanism and Rediscovery

The Renaissance period was a time of rebirth in arts, culture, and science. It teaches us the value of revisiting and learning from past cultures and knowledge, as evidenced by the revival of Greco-Roman philosophies. The era also underlines the importance of humanism and the focus on human potential and creativity.

The Industrial Revolution: Innovation and Its Impacts

The Industrial Revolution brought about massive changes in technology, economy, and society. This period shows us the transformative power of innovation but also warns us about the socio-economic disparities and environmental impacts that can result from unchecked industrial growth.

The World Wars: Conflict and Consequence

The first and second World Wars were pivotal in shaping the modern world. They teach us about the devastating effects of global conflict, the horrors of war, and the importance of international cooperation and peace. These wars also led to significant political, social, and technological changes.

The Cold War and Modern History

The Cold War era, marked by the rivalry between the United States and the Soviet Union, teaches us about the dynamics of power and the dangers of ideological extremism. It also provides lessons on diplomacy, espionage, and the role of nuclear deterrence in maintaining global peace.

Understanding societies provides insight into how societies were formed and evolved. It helps us understand the social, political, and cultural contexts of different communities, fostering a better understanding of diverse cultures and lifestyles.

Identity and Heritage contributes to personal and national identity. Knowing the history of one's country or culture can instill a sense of pride and belonging. It helps in preserving traditions, languages, and stories that define communities.

Studying history encourages analytical and critical thinking. It involves assessing evidence, considering multiple perspectives, and developing reasoned arguments, skills valuable in many aspects of life.

Historical knowledge is crucial for policymakers. Understanding historical contexts can help in creating effective policies and avoiding past mistakes.

History provides a global view, showing how nations and cultures have interacted over time. This perspective is important for fostering global cooperation and understanding in an increasingly interconnected world.

Remembering historical injustices and struggles for rights, history plays a crucial role in the ongoing fight for human rights and justice.

Historical figures and events can inspire individuals and societies. They show resilience in the face of adversity and the potential to effect change.

Cultural exchange and understanding is a bridge to understanding different cultures, helping reduce prejudices and stereotypes.

Learning from Success and Failure

History is replete with examples of both triumph and disaster. The rise and fall of empires, the success or failure of economic systems, and the outcomes of political ideologies provide rich lessons. For instance, the fall of the

Roman Empire offers insights into the dangers of overextension and the importance of stable governance, while the success of the Industrial Revolution illustrates the transformative power of innovation. These historical narratives can guide today's leaders in making informed decisions that avoid past mistakes and emulate successful strategies.

Understanding Cultural and Social Evolution

Recognizing different eras, we gain perspective on how societies evolve. The Renaissance, for example, marked a significant shift in artistic, cultural, and intellectual life, which laid the foundations for modern Western thought. Understanding these shifts helps us appreciate the diversity of human experience and informs our approach to contemporary cultural and social issues.

Technological Advancements and their Historical Context

Technology has been a significant driver of historical change. From the invention of the wheel to the development of the internet, technological advancements have reshaped societies. By studying the historical context of these inventions, we learn not only about the process of innovation but also about the ethical and societal implications that accompany technological progress.

Political and Economic Histories

Knowing political and economic histories is crucial for understanding current global dynamics. The transitions from feudalism to capitalism, the rise of democracy, and the impact of colonialism and imperialism have shaped today's political and economic landscapes. Analyzing these histories offers valuable insights into the strengths and weaknesses of various systems, informing current policy-making and economic strategies.

History of Human Rights and Social Justice

The history of human rights and social justice movements is a testament to the human spirit's resilience and pursuit of equality. From the abolition of slavery to the civil rights movement, these historical struggles provide a blueprint for contemporary social justice efforts. They remind us that progress is possible and that the fight for justice is an ongoing journey.

Environmental History and Sustainability

Our historical relationship with the environment has been complex. Studying environmental history, including the rise of industrialization and its impact on nature, teaches us valuable lessons about sustainability. It highlights the need for a balanced approach to development, one that respects and preserves our natural world for future generations.

History, in its vast expanse, offers unending lessons. From the resilience of ancient civilizations to the transformative impacts of technological advancements, each period provides unique insights. We learn not only about our past but also about the potential paths for our future. The lessons extracted from history should guide us in building a better, more informed, and more compassionate world.

CHAPTER 5
LITERATURE: WINDOWS INTO OTHER WORLDS

I. The Magic of Literature

In the realm of human creativity, literature stands as a towering testament to our capacity for imagination and empathy. It is not merely a collection of words or a play of language; literature is a portal, a window into worlds both real and imagined, a bridge connecting the minds of readers to experiences and places they may never physically encounter.

II. Literature as a Time Machine

Consider the works of historical fiction, where authors meticulously reconstruct eras long gone. Through the pages of a book, readers can walk the cobblestone streets of Victorian London, feel the tension in a Revolutionary War-era American colony, or experience the cultural renaissance of the Harlem Renaissance. Literature, in this sense, acts as a time machine, offering a glimpse into the past, helping us understand where we came from and how our present has been shaped.

III. Cultural Exploration through Stories

Furthermore, literature allows us to cross cultural boundaries. Reading a novel set in a foreign land or written by an author from a different background can be a profoundly enlightening experience. It can shatter stereotypes, build empathy, and offer insights into the lives, traditions, and perspectives of people from around the globe. In reading, we travel mentally, experiencing the diverse tapestry of human life.

IV. Escaping into Fantastical Realms

Fantasy and science fiction take this concept to even greater heights. These genres create entire universes, governed by their own rules and populated with unique beings and societies. From the high fantasy of J.R.R. Tolkien's Middle-earth to the far-flung future of Isaac

Asimov's galactic empires, these worlds, while fictional, offer a space for readers to explore fundamental human questions in settings unbound by the constraints of reality.

V. Reflecting on the Human Condition

At the heart of all literature, whether it be set in a realistic or fantastical world, is the exploration of the human condition. Through characters and their journeys, readers confront and reflect upon themes like love, loss, courage, fear, and morality. In this way, literature does more than just entertain; it enlightens, offering windows into the myriad ways of being human.

VI. The Role of Narrative Styles and Techniques

The way stories are told also contributes to how they act as windows into other worlds. Narrative techniques like stream of consciousness, unreliable narrators, or non-linear timelines can immerse readers in the psychological realities of characters, offering a more intimate and complex view of their worlds. The narrative style, be it poetic, terse, or richly descriptive, colors the lens through which readers view these other worlds.

VII. Literature as a Mirror

Sometimes, the most powerful worlds literature shows us are reflections of our own. In dystopian novels, for instance, we see our societies taken to extremes, highlighting current issues and potential futures. These reflections can be cautionary, illuminating, or even inspiring, prompting readers to think critically about the world they inhabit.

VIII. Bridging the Gap between Generations

Literature also serves as a link between generations. Through stories, the wisdom, experiences, and cultures of the past are passed down, allowing for a dialogue between the ages. This intergenerational exchange enriches our understanding of both the past and the present, creating a continuity of the human experience.

IX. The Personal Worlds within Literature

Each reader's experience of a book is unique. The worlds they enter through literature are colored by their own experiences, thoughts, and emotions. In this way, every act of reading is the creation of a new world, a personal interpretation that lives within the mind of the reader.

X. An Endless Journey

In conclusion, literature's capacity to serve as a window into other worlds is limitless. Each book offers a journey, an escape, an education, and a reflection. As long as there are stories to be told and readers to imagine them, literature will continue to open doors to endless worlds, both real and imagined, offering glimpses into the infinite possibilities of human experience.

screen-printing. Each method has its unique qualities and can be used to create multiple copies of a work.

- **Digital Art:** This is a relatively new genre that uses digital technology as part of the creative or presentation process. It includes digital painting, 3D modeling, and digital installations, and often involves interactive elements.
- **Performance Art:** This is a performance presented to an audience within a fine art context, traditionally interdisciplinary. Performance art often involves the artist, but the performers can be others as well, and the performance can be live or via media.
- **Ceramics:** This refers to items made from clay and hardened by heat. It encompasses fine art objects like figures, tiles, and tableware. The art of ceramics is diverse, ranging from simple earthenware to complex porcelain pieces.
- **Textile Arts:** This involves the use of plant, animal, or synthetic fibers to construct practical or decorative objects. Textiles encompass arts like weaving, knitting, crocheting, and embroidery.

- **Architecture:** While primarily associated with designing and constructing buildings, architecture is also considered an art form because of its focus on aesthetic elements and the creation of spaces that resonate with their inhabitants.
- **Conceptual Art:** This is art in which the ideas or concepts behind the work are more important than the finished art object. It emerged as a movement in the 1960s and often involves a combination of different mediums.
- **Mixed Media:** This refers to artworks that use a combination of materials or techniques. Mixed media art can include the use of paint, ink, paper, wood, textiles, and found objects.
- **Installation Art:** Installation art is a genre in which three-dimensional works are often site-specific and designed to transform the perception of a space. It can include a range of different materials and is often interactive.
- **Folk Art:** Folk art refers to art produced from an indigenous culture or by peasants or other laboring tradespeople. It is characterized by a naive style, in which traditional rules of proportion and perspective are not employed.

- **Abstract Art:** This type of art does not attempt to represent an accurate depiction of visual reality but instead uses shapes, colors, forms, and gestural marks to achieve its effect.

The Historical Evolution of Art and Creativity

Art has been an integral part of human civilization since the dawn of time. From the primitive cave paintings of Lascaux to the intricate sculptures of ancient Greece, and from the Renaissance masterpieces to contemporary digital art, the evolution of art mirrors the evolution of human society. Each era's artistic expressions reflect not only the aesthetic sensibilities of the time but also the cultural, political, and social dynamics. The Renaissance, for example, marked a significant shift in art, highlighting humanism and individual expression, which was a departure from the predominantly religious art of the Middle Ages.

Creativity, on the other hand, is an ancient and enduring human trait that drives this artistic evolution. It is the ability to generate novel and valuable ideas, transcending traditional ways of thinking. Creativity is not confined to the arts; it is evident in every aspect of human endeavor, from science and technology to everyday problem-solving. However, in the realm of art, creativity is the force that challenges norms, pushes boundaries, and introduces new perspectives.

The Psychology of Creative Expression

Creativity is deeply rooted in the human psyche. Psychological theories have long sought to understand the processes behind creative thought. Psychologist J.P. Guilford's theory of divergent thinking, for instance, emphasizes the ability to generate multiple solutions to a problem, a key aspect of creativity. Additionally, the flow state, a concept introduced by Mihaly Csikszentmihalyi, describes a mental state of deep immersion and focus in an activity, often associated with the creative process in art.

Moreover, art as a form of expression can be therapeutic. It provides a conduit for individuals to process and express emotions that are difficult to articulate. This is evident in art therapy practices, where creating art helps individuals deal with trauma, mental health issues, and emotional challenges.

Art as a Universal Language

One of the most profound aspects of art is its ability to transcend linguistic and cultural barriers. Art speaks a universal language, one that can be understood and appreciated regardless of the viewer's background. This universality is evident in the global appreciation of works like Leonardo da Vinci's "Mona Lisa" or Vincent van Gogh's "Starry Night." These works resonate with people worldwide, regardless of their cultural or historical context.

Furthermore, art has the unique ability to capture and convey the human experience. It can express the inexpressible – feelings, thoughts, and experiences that are otherwise difficult to communicate. Through symbolism, metaphor, and abstraction, artists can convey deeper meanings and evoke emotional responses.

CHAPTER 7
PSYCHOLOGY: UNLOCKING THE HUMAN MIND

The human mind, a labyrinth of thoughts, emotions, and memories, has intrigued philosophers, scientists, and thinkers throughout history. Psychology, the scientific study of the mind and behavior, seeks to unlock the secrets of this complex organ, revealing the intricate mechanisms that govern our everyday lives. This chapter delves into the depths of psychological exploration, unraveling the mysteries of cognition, emotion, and the subconscious.

The Foundations of Psychology

The journey into the human mind begins with the roots of psychology. From the philosophical musings of ancient Greece to the scientific rigor of the 19th century, the evolution of psychology has been a blend of introspection and empirical investigation. Pioneers like Wilhelm Wundt and William James laid the groundwork for modern psychological thought, transforming the study of the mind from a philosophical conjecture to a scientific endeavor.

Understanding Cognition

At the heart of psychology lies cognition—the processes of thinking, reasoning, and problem-solving. Cognitive psychology, a branch dedicated to understanding these mental processes, explores how we perceive the world, form memories, and make decisions. Seminal experiments, such as those conducted by Jean Piaget on children's cognitive development, have shed light on how our understanding of the world evolves from infancy to adulthood.

The Realm of Emotions

Emotions, the vivid colors of our mental canvas, play a crucial role in shaping our experiences and behaviors. Psychological theories, from Freud's psychoanalytic perspective to contemporary models of emotional intelligence, have sought to explain the origin and impact of emotions. Research into emotional regulation, resilience, and the connection between emotion and physical health has underscored the profound influence emotions have on our overall well-being.

The Subconscious Mind

Delving deeper into the psyche, the subconscious mind emerges as a mysterious and powerful force. Influenced by the pioneering work of Sigmund Freud and Carl Jung, psychology has explored the realms of dreams, instincts, and the unconscious processes that silently steer our thoughts and actions. The study of the subconscious has not only enriched our understanding of human behavior but also has practical implications in areas like therapy and personal development.

Social Psychology and Interpersonal Dynamics

Humans are inherently social beings, and our interactions with others significantly shape our mental landscape. Social psychology examines how societal norms, group dynamics, and interpersonal relationships influence our thoughts, feelings, and behaviors. From the groundbreaking experiments of Solomon Asch on conformity to the complex theories of attachment and social identity, this field provides insights into the social fabric of our minds.

The Neurobiological Underpinnings

The exploration of the human mind is incomplete without understanding its biological basis. Neuropsychology bridges the gap between psychology and neuroscience, investigating how brain structures and functions give rise to mental processes. Advances in brain imaging technologies, like fMRI and PET scans, have revolutionized our understanding of brain-behavior relationships, illuminating the neural pathways involved in everything from language to emotion.

Abnormal Psychology and Mental Health

One of the most compelling areas of psychological study is abnormal psychology, which focuses on understanding mental disorders and psychological distress. This field not only seeks to classify and diagnose mental illnesses but also aims to understand their causes and develop effective treatments. The importance of mental health has gained increasing recognition, leading to a greater emphasis on therapies, counseling, and public awareness campaigns.

Learning and Behavior Modification

How do humans learn and change their behavior? Behavioral psychology, rooted in the work of B.F. Skinner and John B. Watson, addresses these questions. By studying the principles of conditioning and reinforcement, psychologists have developed methods for behavior modification, applicable in education, parenting, and even self-improvement.

The Impact of Culture and Environment

The mind does not exist in isolation; it is profoundly influenced by cultural and environmental factors. Cross-cultural psychology examines how cultural beliefs and practices shape our mental processes and behaviors. Environmental psychology explores the interaction between individuals and their physical surroundings, shedding light on how our environment impacts our mental health and behavior.

Future Directions in Psychology

As we continue to unlock the mysteries of the human mind, new frontiers in psychology emerge. The integration of technology, like artificial intelligence and virtual reality, is opening up novel approaches to therapy and research. The growing field of positive psychology focuses on human strengths and virtues, shifting the narrative from illness to well-being.

Quest to understand this enigmatic organ, continues to evolve, constantly shedding new light on what it means to be human. As we delve deeper into the realms of thought, emotion, and behavior, we not only gain insights into ourselves but also forge paths toward greater empathy, understanding, and mental well-being. The study of psychology is not just an academic pursuit; it is a journey to the very core of our existence.

CHAPTER 8
TECHNOLOGY: TOOLS FOR TOMORROW

The Dawn of a New Era

In the heart of Silicon Valley, beneath the shadow of towering skyscrapers that glinted like a tableau of modern ambition, a revolution was brewing—a revolution not of conflict, but of creation. The 21st century had ushered in an era of unprecedented technological advancement, a time where the digital and physical realms converged in a symphony of progress. This was a world where technology was no longer a mere tool, but a transformative force, sculpting the future with the hands of innovation.

The Architects of Change

The protagonists of this story were not just the tech moguls and coding prodigies. They were the unsung heroes—the educators, the environmentalists, the healthcare workers—who harnessed these tools to forge a better tomorrow. At the core of their arsenal were three pivotal technologies that promised to redefine the boundaries of human potential: Artificial Intelligence (AI), Quantum Computing, and Biotechnology.

AI: The Mind Beyond the Machine

AI had evolved from a rudimentary tool for data processing into a sophisticated entity capable of decision-making, learning, and even emulating human emotions. It was no longer confined to the realms of science fiction; it had become a tangible, integral part of daily life. From the algorithms that curated personalized news feeds to the virtual assistants that managed homes, AI was a pervasive presence.

In education, AI tutors adapted to each student's learning style, offering a bespoke education that was both inclusive and effective. In healthcare, AI-driven diagnostics predicted diseases before they manifested, revolutionizing preventative medicine. In environmental conservation, AI systems monitored and predicted climate patterns, aiding in the fight against global warming.

Quantum Computing: Unlocking New Realms

Quantum Computing, a marvel of modern physics, operated on the principles of quantum mechanics. It represented a quantum leap from traditional computing, handling complex calculations at speeds previously deemed impossible. This technology had far-reaching implications, from creating new materials to solving intricate scientific problems.

In the field of cryptography, quantum computers offered unparalleled security, creating encryption methods that were impregnable to conventional hacking techniques. In logistics and supply chain management, they optimized routes and inventory, reducing waste and enhancing efficiency. In pharmaceuticals, they enabled the rapid development of new drugs, tailoring treatments to individual genetic profiles.

Biotechnology: The Blueprint of Life

Biotechnology, the frontier of biological exploration, stood at the intersection of biology and technology. It was an ode to the understanding and manipulation of the very fabric of life—DNA. Gene editing techniques, like CRISPR, had the potential to eradicate genetic diseases, while synthetic biology promised to revolutionize food production and medicine.

Agriculture witnessed a transformation with genetically modified crops that were resistant to pests and climate change, ensuring food security. In medicine, personalized treatments based on an individual's genetic makeup became the norm, offering targeted and effective therapies. Biodegradable materials, born from the womb of biotech innovations, offered sustainable alternatives to plastics, reducing environmental footprint.

The Ethical Compass

With great power came great responsibility. The ethical implications of these technologies were a labyrinth of moral and philosophical questions. AI raised concerns about privacy and the potential loss of jobs to automation. Quantum computing, while a boon for security, also posed risks of creating unbreakable codes that could be misused. Biotechnology treaded a fine line between innovation and playing god.

To navigate these challenges, a global coalition of tech leaders, ethicists, and policymakers convened, striving to create a framework that balanced innovation with moral responsibility. Their goal was to ensure that these tools of tomorrow were used for the betterment of humanity, not its detriment.

The Confluence of Human and Machine

As these technologies converged, they created a tapestry of interconnectivity. AI algorithms optimized quantum computer operations, while quantum computing propelled AI into new realms of possibility. Biotechnology benefited from AI's predictive capabilities and quantum computing's data analysis prowess.

This confluence marked the emergence of a new paradigm, where human and machine worked in unison, each augmenting the other's capabilities. It was a symbiosis that transcended traditional boundaries, blurring the lines between biology and technology, the organic and the artificial.

The Ripple Effect

The impact of these technologies extended beyond the confines of labs and boardrooms. They touched every facet of society, reshaping economies, education systems, and social structures. Jobs evolved, requiring new skills and fostering lifelong learning. Healthcare became more accessible and personalized, enhancing the quality of life.

In developing nations, these technologies bridged the digital divide, providing access to information and resources that were previously out of reach. They empowered communities, fostering innovation and entrepreneurship at a grassroots level.

The Vision of Tomorrow

As the sun set over Silicon Valley, casting long shadows across the tech utopia, a vision of the future emerged. It was a world where technology was a catalyst for positive change, a tool that empowered humanity to reach new heights. It was a future that was not feared

CHAPTER 9
ECONOMICS: THE SCIENCE OF SCARCITY AND CHOICE

Often hailed as the science of scarcity and choice, is a realm that intricately weaves through the very fabric of society, shaping the way individuals, governments, and corporations navigate the complex web of resource allocation and decision-making. This chapter delves into the heart of economics, exploring its fundamental concepts, real-world applications, and the profound impact it has on our daily lives.

At its core, economics is the study of how people use their limited resources to satisfy unlimited wants. The concept of scarcity, a cornerstone of economic theory, asserts that resources such as time, money, and materials are finite, while human desires and needs are seemingly endless. This imbalance between limited resources and unlimited wants is the crux of economic inquiry.

The science of economics branches into two critical areas: microeconomics and macroeconomics.

Microeconomics focuses on the behavior of individual consumers and firms, dissecting how they make choices about resource allocation. It examines the dynamics of supply and demand, price mechanisms, and the intricate interplay of factors influencing individual markets.

Macroeconomics looks at the economy as a whole, analyzing aggregate indicators like gross domestic product (GDP), inflation rates, and unemployment to understand the broader economic trends and policies.

One of the most fundamental concepts in economics is the notion of opportunity cost. It refers to the value of the next best alternative foregone as a result of making a decision. This concept highlights the trade-offs involved in every economic choice, whether it's an individual deciding how to spend their time or a government allocating budget resources.

Economic models and theories offer frameworks for understanding the complex interactions and outcomes in a market. The supply and demand model, for instance, illustrates how prices are determined in a market, balancing the quantity of goods supplied by producers and the quantity demanded by consumers. This model also elucidates how external factors, like changes in consumer preferences or production costs, can shift supply and demand curves, leading to new market equilibriums.

In real-world scenarios, market economies are often guided by the invisible hand, a concept introduced by Adam Smith, suggesting that individual self-interest in a free market can lead to societal benefits. However, this ideal scenario is often complicated by market failures, such as monopolies, externalities, and public goods, where unregulated markets fail to allocate resources efficiently or equitably.

Governments intervene in economies to correct these market failures, employing tools like taxation, subsidies, and regulation. For instance, to address negative externalities like pollution, a government might impose a tax on carbon emissions, internalizing the external costs. Similarly, public goods, which are non-excludable and non-rivalrous, like national defense or public parks, are typically provided by the government since they would be underprovided in a purely free market.

Economic policies are often shaped by differing schools of thought. Keynesian economics, for example, advocates for active government intervention, especially during economic downturns, to stimulate demand and pull the economy out of recession. In contrast, classical and neoclassical economists emphasize the self-regulating nature of markets and the importance of limiting government intervention.

Global economics further complicates these dynamics. International trade, globalization, and the interconnectedness of national economies play a pivotal role in shaping economic policies and outcomes. Trade theories, like comparative advantage, explain how countries benefit from specializing in the production of goods and services they can produce most efficiently and trading for others.

In recent years, behavioral economics has emerged, challenging the traditional assumption of rational decision-making in classical economics. It integrates insights from psychology to understand how cognitive biases and emotions influence economic decisions, offering a more nuanced view of human behavior in economic contexts.

Sustainable economics is another growing field, emphasizing the need to balance economic growth with environmental sustainability and social equity. This perspective is increasingly relevant as the world grapples with challenges like climate change, resource depletion, and widening inequality.

This fundamental tension drives economic activity and decision-making across the globe. Understanding economics is not just about grasping theories; it's about applying these concepts to generate wealth and improve living standards.

The Essence of Wealth Generation

Generating wealth in an economy hinges on several key principles. Firstly, wealth is not merely about accumulating money; it's about creating value. This value can be in the form of goods, services, or innovations that improve lives. Economies grow when they efficiently convert resources (like labor, capital, and raw materials) into valuable outputs.

Investment and Capital Formation

One of the primary drivers of wealth generation is investment. Investing in physical capital (like machinery and infrastructure) and human capital (education and skills) boosts productivity. A more productive economy can produce more goods and services with the same amount of resources, leading to higher income and wealth.

Innovation and Technology

Innovation is a critical wealth generator. Technological advancements can lead to new products, improve processes, and open up fresh markets. The digital revolution, for instance, has spawned industries that didn't exist a few decades ago, creating immense wealth and transforming societies.

Trade and Globalization

Trade is a powerful engine for wealth creation. By specializing in products or services they can produce most efficiently and trading for others, countries can enhance their overall wealth. Globalization has interconnected markets, allowing for the flow of goods, services, capital, and labor across borders, further boosting wealth potential.

Effective Governance and Economic Policies

The role of governments and institutions is pivotal in shaping economic outcomes. Sound fiscal and monetary policies can stabilize an economy, encourage investment, and foster an environment conducive to wealth generation. Regulations are necessary to maintain fair competition, protect property rights, and ensure the efficient functioning of markets.

Challenges and Sustainability

While pursuing wealth generation, economies face challenges like income inequality, environmental degradation, and resource depletion. Sustainable economic growth, which balances current needs with those of future generations, is becoming increasingly important. This involves addressing climate change, investing in renewable energy, and ensuring equitable growth.

Economics is not just a dry science of numbers and graphs; it's a vibrant field that touches every aspect of our lives. From the personal choices we make every day to the sweeping policies that shape national economies, economics offers a lens through which we can understand and navigate the world around us. It teaches us about the trade-offs we face, the consequences of our decisions, and the complex interdependencies that bind us together in a globalized world. As we continue to confront new challenges and opportunities, the principles and insights of economics will remain invaluable in guiding our choices and shaping a better future.

CHAPTER 10
POLITICS AND GOVERNANCE: POWER IN PRACTICE

In the grand theater of politics and governance, power unfolds like an intricate dance, choreographed within the complex interplay of ambition, ideology, and the relentless pursuit of control. It is a realm where every gesture, every word, and every alliance is a deliberate step in the dance of domination and influence.

As dawn breaks over the capital city, the corridors of power awaken to the rhythmic pulse of ambition. The city, a microcosm of political intrigue, is a maze of opulent government buildings, bustling cafés, and serene parks, each a stage for the subtle maneuvers of power. Here, politicians, bureaucrats, activists, and lobbyists converge, their paths intertwining in the pursuit of influence.

In the heart of the city, the grand legislature stands as a symbol of democratic governance. Its marble halls echo with the voices of elected representatives, each carrying the weight of their constituents' hopes and grievances. Here, the dance of democracy unfolds, a complex ballet of debate, negotiation, and compromise. Laws are crafted not just with pen and paper, but through the intricate waltz of political alliances and rivalries.

Within these hallowed halls, one can observe the seasoned politician, a master of the craft, weaving through the crowd with a calculated grace. Their every handshake, every smile, a meticulously crafted display of camaraderie and charm. They listen intently, speak persuasively, and move strategically, always aware of the shifting tides of political favor.

Yet, the dance of power extends far beyond these walls. In the shadowed corners of the city, where the glimmer of cameras fades, power takes on a more elusive form. Here, in the quiet meeting rooms of luxury hotels and the private dining rooms of exclusive clubs, decisions are made that will never reach the public ear. Deals are struck, promises exchanged, and alliances formed in hushed tones. This is the unseen ballet of power, where influence is traded like currency, and the stakes are as high as the positions of those who dance.

The media, with its ever-watchful eye, plays a pivotal role in this dance. Reporters, armed with questions like sharpened swords, seek to expose the hidden steps of the powerful. In response, politicians don intricate masks of rhetoric and deflection, performing a delicate dance of disclosure and secrecy. The relationship between the media and the government is a complex tango of mutual dependence and cautious distrust.

In the midst of this political landscape, the voice of the people resounds like a powerful chorus. Protests and rallies fill the streets, their chants and banners painting a vivid picture of public opinion and dissent. Here, the power of the masses is palpable, a reminder that in a democracy, true power ultimately lies in the hands of the governed.

Yet, power is not immune to corruption. In the darker corners of governance, where oversight wanes, the seductive whisper of corruption lures the unwary. Bribes, scandals, and abuses of power are the missteps in the dance, threatening to disrupt the delicate balance of governance. It is a constant battle to maintain integrity within the alluring embrace of power.

Amidst this intricate dance, the role of ethics and morality becomes paramount. For those who govern, the challenge is to navigate the complex waters of politics without losing sight of their moral compass. They must balance ambition with responsibility, authority with compassion, and power with humility.

As the sun sets over the capital, the dance of power slows, but it never truly stops. In the quiet of the night, strategies are devised, plans are laid, and the dance continues, ever-evolving. Politics and governance are not just about the exercise of power; they are about its stewardship. The true art of this dance lies not in the attainment of power, but in its wise and just application.

In this ever-shifting landscape, one truth remains constant: power, in its essence, is not just about ruling over others. It is about leading, inspiring, and making decisions that will shape the future. It is about the courage to stand for what is right, the wisdom to listen, and the humility to admit mistakes. The intricate dance of power, with all its complexities and challenges, is ultimately a dance of service to the people, a dance that shapes the destiny of nations.

CHAPTER 11
ETHICS AND MORALITY: THE COMPASS FOR ACTION

Ethics and morality are the vibrant threads that add depth and color to the human condition. They are the compasses that guide us through the labyrinth of life's choices, shaping our actions and defining our legacies. This chapter delves into the intricate relationship between ethics and morality, exploring how they influence our decisions and actions, and ultimately, how they shape the world we live in.

The Foundation of Ethics and Morality

At the core, ethics and morality are about discerning right from wrong. But they are more than just societal rules or religious edicts; they are the essence of our humanity. Ethics, derived from the Greek word 'ethos,' refers to a set of principles or values guiding behavior. It is often associated with professional conduct and societal norms, acting as a societal compass. Morality, from the Latin 'moralis,' pertains to personal beliefs and values, a compass that guides individual behavior.

The Moral Compass

Every day, we are faced with choices, some trivial, others life-altering. It is our moral compass that guides these decisions, influenced by cultural, religious, and philosophical teachings. This compass is not static; it evolves as we journey through life, shaped by experiences and reflections. It's a deeply personal aspect, unique to each individual, yet universally understood in its quest for goodness and justice.

The Social Navigator

While morality is personal, ethics are communal. They are the rules and standards set by societies, professions, or organizations to ensure fair and harmonious coexistence. Ethical standards are like the signposts of society, directing collective behavior and helping maintain social order. They evolve too, adapting to societal changes and advancements, reflecting the collective consciousness of the times.

The Interplay of Ethics and Morality

Ethics and morality, while distinct, are deeply intertwined. Personal morality influences societal ethics, and societal ethics shape personal morality. This dynamic interplay is crucial in understanding the complexities of human behavior. For instance, a person's moral belief in honesty shapes their ethical conduct in professional settings, while societal ethics against discrimination influence an individual's moral stance on equality.

Ethical Dilemmas and Moral Quandaries

Life often presents situations where ethics and morality clash, leading to dilemmas and quandaries. These are moments of profound introspection and decision-making, where what is legally or socially acceptable may not align with personal moral beliefs. Navigating these conflicts is a challenging yet essential part of the human experience, requiring empathy, wisdom, and often, courage.

The Role of Ethics and Morality in Leadership

Leaders, be they in government, business, or community roles, wield significant influence. Their actions, driven by their ethical and moral compasses, have far-reaching impacts. Ethical leadership is about making decisions that are not just profitable or politically advantageous, but also morally sound and socially responsible. It's about leading by example, setting a standard for ethical and moral conduct.

Ethics and Morality in a Globalized World

In our interconnected world, the significance of ethics and morality is more pronounced than ever. Global challenges like climate change, economic inequality, and human rights issues demand a unified ethical and moral response. This global perspective transcends national, cultural, and religious boundaries, advocating for a collective human conscience.

The Future of Ethics and Morality

As we advance into the future, the conversation around ethics and morality becomes increasingly complex.

Technological advancements, such as artificial intelligence, pose new ethical questions. The moral implications of climate change, genetic engineering, and digital privacy are hotbeds of debate. The future will require a reimagining of our ethical and moral frameworks, adapting them to the changing landscapes of human existence.

Personal Development and Moral Growth

Ethical and moral development is a lifelong process. It involves constant learning, introspection, and adaptation. Engaging in diverse experiences, empathetic interactions, and continuous education enriches our moral and ethical understanding. This personal growth not only benefits the individual but also contributes to a more ethical and moral society.

Living with Ethical and Moral Integrity

Living a life guided by ethics and morality is about aligning actions with values. It's about making choices that are not just beneficial for oneself, but also for the greater good. Ethical and moral integrity involves being honest, responsible, and compassionate. It's about being a beacon of light in a world often clouded by ambiguity and conflict.

Ethics and morality are more than concepts; they are the guiding stars in the journey of life. They shape our actions, influence our decisions, and define our character. As we navigate the complexities of the world, let us hold fast to our ethical and moral compasses, for they are the beacons that light the path to a just, harmonious, and enlightened world.

CHAPTER 12
ENVIRONMENTAL STUDIES: THE PLANET WE CALL HOME

In the heart of our vast and mysterious universe lies a unique and vibrant planet, Earth, our home. It is a world teeming with life, a jewel of biodiversity and natural beauty, and a testament to the resilience and complexity of nature. This chapter delves into the intricate and profound connection we share with our planet, exploring the delicate balance of ecosystems, the impact of human activities, and the urgent need for environmental stewardship.

The Majesty of Earth's Ecosystems

Our planet is a mosaic of diverse ecosystems, each a symphony of life and natural processes. From the sprawling rainforests, the lungs of our planet, to the deep, mysterious oceans teeming with life, Earth's ecosystems are intricate networks where plants, animals, and microorganisms interact in a delicate balance. These ecosystems are not just collections of living organisms; they are interdependent systems where the physical environment, such as climate, soil, and water, plays a crucial role.

The Circle of Life: Biodiversity and its Significance

Biodiversity, the variety of life on Earth, is one of our planet's greatest treasures. It ranges from the smallest microbe to the largest mammal, each organism playing a vital role in the tapestry of life. Biodiversity is not just about the number of species; it's about their variability and the ecological functions they perform. It is this diversity that makes ecosystems resilient, helps them recover from disturbances, and provides us with essential services like clean air, water, and fertile soil.

Climate: The Rhythms of Our World

The Earth's climate is a complex system, influenced by the sun, the atmosphere, the oceans, and land surfaces.

It shapes our environments and influences the distribution of life on Earth. Climate patterns have always been dynamic, but human-induced climate change is altering these patterns at an unprecedented rate. The consequences are profound, affecting everything from weather patterns to sea levels, and consequently, the habitats and survival of many species.

Human Footprints: Our Impact on the Planet

Humanity's relationship with the environment has evolved over millennia. From hunter-gatherers who lived in harmony with nature to the industrial age, where exploitation of natural resources became the norm, our impact on the planet has been profound. Deforestation, pollution, overfishing, and greenhouse gas emissions are just a few examples of how human activities are affecting the Earth's ecosystems and contributing to environmental degradation.

Water: The Source of Life

Water is fundamental to life on Earth. Oceans, rivers, lakes, and groundwater systems provide habitats, regulate climate, and are a source of sustenance and recreation. However, water is also a resource under threat. Pollution, overuse, and climate change are impacting water quality and availability, posing challenges for all life forms that depend on it.

The Soil Beneath Our Feet

Soil is often overlooked, but it is a critical component of our planet's ecosystem. It supports plant growth, stores carbon, and is a habitat for countless organisms. Soil health is vital for food production and ecosystem services. However, practices like deforestation, overgrazing, and chemical pollution are degrading soil at an alarming rate, threatening food security and natural ecosystems.

The Call of the Wild: Wildlife Conservation

Earth's wildlife is a marvel of evolution, but many species are now at risk due to human activities. Habitat destruction, poaching, and climate change are driving species towards extinction. Wildlife conservation efforts are crucial to protect these species and maintain the balance of ecosystems. This involves not just protecting individual species, but also preserving their habitats and addressing the root causes of their decline.

The Urban Challenge: Sustainable Cities

As the world becomes increasingly urbanized, cities face unique environmental challenges. Pollution, waste management, and energy consumption are just a few of the issues that need to be addressed to make cities sustainable. Urban planning that incorporates green spaces, sustainable transport, and energy-efficient buildings is essential for reducing the environmental footprint of cities.

Renewable Energy: Powering a Sustainable Future

The shift from fossil fuels to renewable energy is essential for mitigating climate change. Solar, wind, hydro, and geothermal energy are cleaner and more sustainable sources of power. Investing in renewable energy technologies not only reduces greenhouse gas emissions but also creates new industries and job opportunities.

The Role of Individuals: Making a Difference

Each of us has a role to play in protecting our planet. Simple actions like reducing waste, conserving water, using public transport, and supporting sustainable products can have a significant impact. Education and awareness are key to fostering a culture of environmental stewardship, where each individual understands their impact on the planet and takes steps to reduce it.

The Path Forward: Environmental Policies and Global Cooperation

Addressing environmental challenges requires strong policies and global cooperation. International agreements like the Paris Climate Accord are essential for setting targets and encouraging countries to reduce their environmental impact. However, policies need to be backed by action at the national and local levels, with governments, businesses, and communities working together towards a sustainable future.

A Vision for the Future

Our planet is at a crossroads. The decisions we make today will shape the future of Earth and all its inhabitants. By understanding our planet's systems, respecting its limits, and working together, we can create a sustainable future. It's a future where humans live in harmony with nature, where the air is clean, the water is pure, and the Earth thrives. This is the legacy we can leave for future generations, a testament to our ability to rise to the challenges and ensure the survival and prosperity of our home, planet Earth.

CHAPTER 13
SOCIAL JUSTICE: FOSTERING EQUALITY AND FAIRNESS

In the heart of a bustling metropolis, where skyscrapers cast long shadows over the avenues, the concept of social justice often seems like a distant ideal, lost amidst the cacophony of daily life. Yet, it remains an omnipresent force, silently weaving through the lives of millions, seeking to mend the fissures created by inequality and unfairness. Social justice, in its essence, is the pursuit of a society where every individual, regardless of their background, has equal access to opportunities, resources, and rights. It's a journey towards a future where the scales of justice do not tip in favor of the privileged few but stand balanced for all.

The Roots of Inequality

To understand social justice, one must first grasp the deep-rooted inequalities that pervade our society. These inequalities manifest in various forms - economic disparity, racial and gender discrimination, unequal access to education and healthcare, and the marginalization of minority communities. Each of these issues, like threads in a tapestry, intertwine to create a complex picture of social injustice.

In the shadow of these towering issues, the lives of the underprivileged often go unnoticed. Their struggles are as diverse as their backgrounds - a single mother working two jobs to feed her children, a young immigrant facing the harsh winds of discrimination, or an elderly man unable to afford necessary healthcare. Their stories, though different, share a common theme - a battle against the unjust structures of society.

The Pillars of Social Justice

Social justice stands on four foundational pillars - equity, access, participation, and rights. Equity involves ensuring fairness and justice in the distribution of resources and opportunities. It's not merely about equality, where everyone gets the same, but about tailor-making solutions to ensure everyone gets what they need to succeed.

Access is about removing barriers that prevent people from utilizing resources and opportunities. This can range from providing ramps for wheelchair users to ensuring that education is affordable and accessible to all.

Participation is the empowerment of all members of society to have a voice in the decisions that affect their lives. It's about creating platforms where the marginalized can speak and be heard, where their opinions matter and influence change.

Rights are the legal and moral entitlements that every individual should have, regardless of their status. This includes the right to free speech, the right to a fair trial, and the right to education and healthcare.

The Role of Education in Fostering Social Justice

Education plays a pivotal role in fostering social justice. It is both a tool for personal empowerment and a means to challenge and change unfair systems. An educated populace is more likely to understand their rights and stand up against injustices. Education broadens perspectives, enabling individuals to appreciate and respect diversity. It equips people with the skills needed to participate effectively in society and make informed decisions.

The Challenge of Implementation

However, the road to achieving social justice is fraught with challenges. The most significant of these is resistance to change. Societal structures and norms that have been in place for generations are not easily altered. Those who benefit from the status quo often resist efforts to bring about change, fearing the loss of their privileged position.

Another challenge is the complexity of the issues at hand. Problems like poverty, racism, and gender inequality are deeply intertwined and cannot be solved in isolation. Each requires a comprehensive approach that addresses the root causes and not just the symptoms.

The Agents of Change

In the quest for social justice, various actors play crucial roles. Governments, through policy-making and legislation, have the power to enact changes that promote fairness and equality. Non-governmental organizations and activists act as watchdogs and advocates, pushing for reforms and holding those in power accountable.

However, the most significant agents of change are ordinary people. Social justice is not just the responsibility of governments and organizations; it's a collective duty that falls on the shoulders of every individual. It's about the choices we make daily - the way we treat others, the products we buy, the causes we support.

The Power of Collective Action

The journey towards social justice is long and arduous, but it's a journey that becomes more manageable when traveled together. Collective action has the power to bring about significant change. This can be seen in the various social movements that have shaped our world - the Civil Rights Movement, the fight for women's suffrage, and the recent global movements for climate justice and racial equality.

A Future Envisioned

As the sun sets over the city, casting a golden hue over the streets, one can dream of a future where social justice is not just an ideal but a reality. It's a future where the wealth of opportunities is not hoarded but shared, where differences are celebrated, not discriminated against, where every voice is heard, and every life valued.

This future is achievable, but it requires commitment, courage, and compassion. It calls for a willingness to understand, to empathize, and to act. Social justice is not just a destination but a journey – a continuous process of learning, growing, and improving. It's a path that we all must walk, bridges that we must build, towards a world of balance, equality, and fairness.

CHAPTER 14
HEALTH AND WELLNESS: THE BODY AND MIND CONNECTION

Health and wellness are concepts often discussed in isolation, as if they are separate entities. However, a deeper exploration reveals a profound interconnectedness between the physical body and the mind. This chapter delves into this intricate relationship, unraveling how physical health impacts mental well-being and vice versa, leading to a holistic understanding of health.

Understanding the Body-Mind Connection

The idea that the mind and body are interconnected is far from new. Ancient systems of medicine, such as

Ayurveda and Traditional Chinese Medicine, have long acknowledged this connection. Modern science, too, is beginning to understand this interplay through psychoneuroimmunology – the study of how the mind, nervous system, and immune system interact.

The Impact of Mental Health on Physical Well-being

Mental health significantly impacts physical health. Chronic stress, for example, can lead to a host of physical ailments. When the body is under stress, it releases hormones like cortisol and adrenaline, which are beneficial in short bursts but detrimental in the long term. Prolonged exposure to these hormones can lead to increased risk of heart disease, hypertension, and a weakened immune system.

Depression and anxiety can also manifest physically. They can disrupt sleep patterns, lead to changes in appetite, and increase the risk of chronic diseases like diabetes and heart conditions. Moreover, mental health disorders can impact the body's pain response, making individuals more sensitive to physical pain.

Physical Health's Influence on Mental State

Conversely, physical health can profoundly influence mental well-being. Regular physical activity is known to reduce symptoms of depression and anxiety. Exercise releases endorphins, often referred to as the body's natural antidepressants. It also helps regulate the body's sleep cycles, which is crucial for mental health.

Nutrition plays a significant role as well. A diet rich in essential nutrients supports brain function, impacting mood and cognitive abilities. For instance, omega-3 fatty acids, found in fish and flaxseeds, are known to reduce symptoms of depression.

Case Studies: Illustrating the Connection

Story of a Marathon Runner

Consider the story of Seth, a marathon runner. Seth began running as a way to cope with anxiety. The more he ran, the more he found his anxiety symptoms diminishing. The physical exertion of running released endorphins, which improved his mood. Furthermore, the discipline and goal-setting involved in marathon training provided a mental focus that helped reduce his anxiety.

The Journey of a Yoga Practitioner

Tiffany, a yoga practitioner, offers another perspective. Initially drawn to yoga for its physical benefits, she soon discovered its mental health advantages. The mindfulness and breathing techniques practiced in yoga helped her manage stress and improved her overall emotional well-being.

The Role of Healthcare in Addressing the Connection

Modern healthcare is increasingly acknowledging the body-mind connection. This holistic approach is evident in treatments that combine physical and mental health interventions. For instance, patients with chronic pain are often provided a combination of physical therapy and counseling to address both the physical and psychological aspects of their pain.

Lifestyle Changes for a Balanced Body-Mind

Physical Activity

Incorporating regular physical activity into one's lifestyle is crucial. It doesn't have to be intense; even moderate activities like walking or swimming can have significant benefits.

Mindfulness and Meditation

Practices like mindfulness and meditation can help in managing stress and improving mental health. These practices encourage a state of present-moment awareness, which can lead to a decrease in stress and anxiety.

Balanced Diet

A balanced diet, rich in nutrients, supports both physical and mental health. Foods that are particularly beneficial for the brain include those rich in omega-3 fatty acids, antioxidants, and vitamins.

Adequate Sleep

Getting enough sleep is essential for both mental and physical health. Sleep helps in the healing and repair of the heart and blood vessels and is crucial for cognitive functions like memory and learning.

Challenges and Future Directions

While the importance of the body-mind connection is increasingly recognized, there remain challenges. One significant challenge is the compartmentalization of healthcare, where mental and physical health are often treated separately. There is a need for more integrated care approaches.

Additionally, societal stigma around mental health continues to be a barrier. This stigma can prevent people from seeking help, thereby exacerbating their physical and mental health issues.

The future of health and wellness lies in a more integrated approach, one that equally values physical and mental health. Research in areas like psychoneuroimmunology is paving the way for this. There is also a growing emphasis on preventive care, emphasizing lifestyle changes that support both physical and mental health.

Acknowledging the impact of mental health on the physical body and vice versa, and by adopting lifestyle changes that support both, individuals can achieve a greater sense of overall health and wellness. As society and healthcare systems evolve to recognize this connection, we move closer to a more comprehensive and effective approach to health.

CHAPTER 15
COMMUNICATION: BRIDGING MINDS AND IDEAS

In a world teeming with diverse thoughts, beliefs, and cultures, communication stands as the bridge that connects the myriad islands of human experience. This chapter delves into the intricate art of communication, exploring its multifaceted role in bridging minds and ideas, fostering understanding, and creating a tapestry of shared human experience.

The Essence of Communication

At its core, communication is more than the mere exchange of words; it is the art of conveying thoughts, feelings, and ideas from one mind to another. It is a dance of expression and reception, where each gesture, word, and tone plays a vital role. This intricate process involves not just speaking, but listening, not just hearing, but understanding.

The History and Evolution of Communication

Tracing back to the dawn of humanity, communication has evolved from primal grunts and gestures to sophisticated languages, both spoken and written. The invention of writing marked a pivotal moment, allowing ideas to transcend time and space, preserved on scrolls and pages. In the digital age, this evolution has accelerated, bridging vast distances instantaneously through the internet and social media, making the world a smaller, more connected place.

The Language of Emotion

Beyond words, communication is deeply rooted in the language of emotion. A smile, a frown, a tear – these universal expressions convey meanings that transcend linguistic barriers, forming a silent dialogue that resonates with our shared humanity. Emotion colors our words, giving them depth and context, and is essential in understanding the true intent behind a message.

The Power of Non-Verbal Communication

Non-verbal cues, such as body language, tone of voice, and facial expressions, are integral to communication. They often convey more than words themselves, revealing unspoken truths and intentions. Understanding these subtle signals is key to grasping the full message, leading to more effective and empathetic interactions.

Cultural Variations in Communication

Culture shapes the way we communicate. From the directness of Western communication to the more subtle and indirect approaches in Eastern cultures, understanding these differences is crucial in an increasingly globalized world. Misunderstandings arise not just from language barriers, but from unmet expectations rooted in cultural norms.

The Digital Communication Revolution

The advent of the internet and social media has revolutionized communication, allowing ideas to spread at an unprecedented rate. This digital landscape offers immense opportunities for learning and connection, but also poses challenges such as information overload, digital miscommunication, and the erosion of privacy.

The Challenges of Effective Communication

Effective communication is not without its obstacles. Language barriers, personal biases, and differing communication styles can lead to misunderstandings and conflict. Overcoming these challenges requires patience, openness, and a willingness to understand and adapt to different perspectives.

The Art of Listening

Listening is half of the communication equation. Active listening involves fully engaging with the speaker, understanding their message, and responding thoughtfully. It is a skill that builds trust and empathy, essential for meaningful dialogue and conflict resolution.

Communication in Relationships

In personal relationships, communication is the lifeline that maintains connection and resolves conflicts. Open, honest, and respectful dialogue fosters deeper understanding and intimacy, strengthening the bonds that tie us to one another.

Communication in the Workplace

In the professional realm, effective communication is key to teamwork, leadership, and productivity. Clear, concise communication ensures that objectives are understood and met, while poor communication can lead to errors, misunderstandings, and a toxic work environment.

The Role of Technology in Communication

Technology has transformed the way we communicate, offering new tools and platforms. However, it also brings challenges such as the loss of face-to-face interaction and the nuances that come with it. Balancing technological convenience with personal connection is the challenge of the modern age.

The Future of Communication

As we look to the future, communication will continue to evolve with technological advancements. Virtual reality, artificial intelligence, and other emerging technologies hold the promise of even more immersive and instant communication. However, the heart of communication will always remain human connection – the timeless art of bridging minds and ideas.

CHAPTER 16
WORLD RELIGIONS: DIVERSE PATHS TO MEANING

The Roots of Religion

Religion, in its essence, is humanity's response to the fundamental questions of existence. From ancient times, humans have sought answers to the nature of life, death, and the forces that govern the universe. This quest has given birth to a multitude of religious expressions, each rooted in the cultural, historical, and geographical contexts of their origin.

The Dharmic Path: Hinduism and Buddhism

In the Indian subcontinent, two of the world's oldest religions, Hinduism and Buddhism, emerged.

Hinduism, with its vast pantheon of deities and deeply philosophical texts like the Bhagavad Gita, offers a diverse range of practices and beliefs. It teaches the concepts of Dharma (duty/righteousness), Karma (action and consequence), and Moksha (liberation from the cycle of rebirth).

Buddhism, founded by Siddhartha Gautama, the Buddha, presents a path centered around the Four Noble Truths and the Eightfold Path. It emphasizes the impermanence of life, the cessation of suffering through detachment from desires, and the attainment of Nirvana.

The Abrahamic Traditions: Judaism, Christianity, and Islam

In the Middle East, three major monotheistic religions emerged: Judaism, Christianity, and Islam. Judaism, one of the oldest monotheistic religions, is rooted in the covenant between God and Abraham and the laws given to Moses. The Torah and the Talmud form the core of Jewish belief and practice.

Christianity, born from the teachings of Jesus Christ, centers on the belief in Jesus as the Son of God and the savior of humanity. The Bible, comprising the Old and

New Testaments, is the holy scripture of Christians, guiding their faith and practice.

Islam, founded by Prophet Muhammad in the 7th century CE, is based on the Quran, considered the verbatim word of God (Allah). Muslims follow the Five Pillars of Islam, including the declaration of faith, prayer, almsgiving, fasting during Ramadan, and the pilgrimage to Mecca.

The Indigenous and Nature-Centric Beliefs

Across the globe, indigenous religions offer a window into the profound connection between humans and the natural world. These belief systems, often animistic, view the natural world as filled with spirits and emphasize the importance of maintaining a harmonious relationship with the environment. From the shamanic traditions of Siberia to the Dreamtime stories of the Australian Aboriginals, these religions highlight the diversity of human spirituality.

The Philosophical and Modern Movements

Religion is not static, and over the centuries, new movements have emerged. Sikhism, founded by Guru Nanak in the 15th century in South Asia, emphasizes the oneness of God and the equality of all humans. Baha'i Faith, a more recent religion, advocates for universal peace and unity among all races, religions, and nations.

In the contemporary world, interfaith dialogue and secular philosophies also contribute to the spiritual landscape. Humanism, for instance, focuses on human values and ethics without necessarily invoking a deity.

The Role of Rituals and Festivals

Rituals and festivals are vibrant expressions of religious beliefs. They range from the Hindu festival of Diwali, celebrating the triumph of light over darkness, to the solemn Christian observance of Lent leading to Easter, commemorating the resurrection of Jesus. These events not only mark important religious milestones but also foster a sense of community and shared identity.

The Art and Architecture of Faith

Religious art and architecture are powerful expressions of faith and devotion. The intricate Islamic calligraphy, the awe-inspiring Christian cathedrals, the serene Buddhist temples, and the majestic Hindu mandirs are not just places of worship but also repositories of history, culture, and art.

Challenges and Transformations

In today's globalized world, religions face numerous challenges. Issues like extremism, the conflict between science and faith, and the quest for relevance in a rapidly changing world are at the forefront. Yet, these challenges also spur transformations within religions, leading to new interpretations and practices that resonate with contemporary adherents.

CHAPTER 17
EMOTIONAL INTELLIGENCE: THE OTHER SIDE OF SMART

Often overlooked aspect of intelligence that transcends the conventional realms of academic prowess and logical reasoning. This facet, known as Emotional Intelligence (EI), is the unspoken language of the heart, the silent dialogue of feelings, and the unique ability to navigate the tumultuous sea of human emotions with grace and understanding.

Emotional Intelligence, in its essence, is the capability to recognize, comprehend, manage, and harness emotions in oneself and others. It's a skill, subtle yet powerful, that allows individuals to empathize, communicate effectively, overcome challenges, and defuse conflict. Unlike the traditional quotient of intelligence – IQ, which measures cognitive abilities, EI delves into the deeper layers of human interaction and self-awareness.

The journey into the world of Emotional Intelligence begins with self-awareness. It is the cornerstone of EI, the intimate understanding of one's emotions, strengths, weaknesses, drives, and capabilities. It's like holding a mirror to one's soul, seeing the reflections of inner emotions and recognizing how they influence thoughts and actions. A person with high self-awareness understands their emotional state and can discern how these emotions and their accompanying behaviors can affect people around them.

Branching out from self-awareness is self-regulation. This component of EI involves controlling or redirecting one's disruptive emotions and adapting to changing circumstances. Imagine the calm before the storm; the ability to maintain tranquility in the face of adversity. It's about expressing feelings appropriately, not suppressing them, and having the flexibility to react to life's surprises with a level head.

A pivotal element of Emotional Intelligence is motivation. Individuals with high EI are generally highly motivated, willing to defer immediate results for long-term success. They are driven by a deep-seated passion to achieve for the sake of achievement. This intrinsic motivation isn't driven by external rewards but rather by an inner ambition and love for what they are doing.

The fourth dimension of EI is empathy. More than just recognizing or understanding others' feelings, empathy is the ability to put oneself in another's shoes, to experience their emotions. In this respect, empathy is a bridge connecting people, fostering deeper connections and understanding. It's the vital ingredient for effective communication, building relationships, and leading successfully.

Lastly, social skills or social intelligence, a component of EI, is about managing relationships to move people in desired directions. This involves effective communication, inspiring and influencing others, conflict management, and nurturing relationships. It's the art of being socially aware, understanding social dynamics, and being able to find common ground and build rapport.

Emotional Intelligence transcends the traditional understanding of intelligence. It's not just about how much someone knows or how well they can solve puzzles but about how they manage their own emotions and perceive those of others. In the complex tapestry of human interactions, EI is the thread that weaves through every communication, every relationship, and every decision.

The importance of Emotional Intelligence in the modern world cannot be overstated. In a rapidly changing, interconnected world, the ability to navigate and harness emotions effectively is invaluable. It enhances leadership capabilities, improves personal and professional relationships, and promotes mental well-being. It's the other side of being smart – the side that balances the scales of human intellect and emotion, creating a more empathetic, understanding, and effective society.

The beauty of EI lies in its universality and its impact; it is a skill that can be developed and refined throughout one's life, contributing not only to personal growth but also to the betterment of society. As the world evolves, Emotional Intelligence stands as a testament to the enduring power of human emotions and the profound impact they have on our lives. It is, indeed, the other side of smart – a side that is equally important and profoundly transformative.

CHAPTER 18
GENDER STUDIES: BEYOND BINARY PERSPECTIVES

In the ever-evolving landscape of human identity and expression, the field of gender studies has emerged as a vibrant and essential discipline, striving to understand the complex tapestry of gender identity and expression beyond the traditional binary framework. This chapter delves into the multifaceted aspects of gender, exploring how cultural, biological, psychological, and social factors intersect to form a more inclusive and nuanced understanding of gender.

Tracing the historical roots of gender studies, highlighting how early feminist and queer theorists challenged the rigid, binary conceptions of gender that dominated societal norms. It examines the groundbreaking work of scholars like Judith Butler, whose theories on gender performativity revolutionized the understanding of gender as a fluid and socially constructed phenomenon. This exploration serves as a foundation for understanding the evolution of gender studies and its departure from traditional binary perspectives.

Complexity of human biology, which does not always fit neatly into the categories of "male" and "female." Intersex conditions, hormonal variations, and chromosomal diversity are explored to illustrate the biological spectrum of gender. This section underscores the importance of recognizing and respecting the natural diversity that exists within human physiology.

The narrative then shifts to the cultural dimensions of gender. It examines how different societies and cultures conceive of gender in varied ways, offering a broader perspective on gender identity and roles. The chapter highlights examples from various cultures around the world, including the "Two-Spirit" individuals in some Indigenous North American cultures and the "Hijras" of South Asia. These examples illuminate how gender is a cultural construct, deeply embedded in the traditions, beliefs, and values of a society.

Psychological aspects of gender form the next focal point of the chapter. It explores how individual experiences and perceptions shape one's understanding of their gender. Personal narratives and psychological theories are employed to discuss topics such as gender dysphoria, transgender experiences, and the journey of self-discovery and affirmation that many individuals undergo in understanding their gender identity.

Examine the challenges and opportunities that arise in various social institutions, including education, healthcare, and the workplace. This section highlights the importance of inclusive policies and practices that acknowledge and accommodate the diverse spectrum of gender identities. It also discusses the role of allies and advocates in fostering a more inclusive and understanding society.

An important aspect of the chapter is the discussion on language and its role in shaping perceptions of gender. The emergence of gender-neutral pronouns and the evolving vocabulary surrounding gender identity are explored to underscore the significance of language in affirming and respecting diverse gender identities.

Ongoing nature of the conversation surrounding gender. It calls for continued exploration, open-mindedness, and empathy in understanding the complexities of gender identity and expression. The chapter ends with a reflection on the importance of education and dialogue in breaking down stereotypes and fostering a society that embraces gender diversity in all its forms.

CHAPTER 19
EDUCATION: THE LIFELONG JOURNEY

In the golden glow of dawn, where the first rays of the sun gently kissed the earth, there began the most profound journey of all – the lifelong pursuit of education. This journey, unlike any other, starts at the cradle and stretches to the far reaches of our final days. It is a voyage that transcends the boundaries of traditional classrooms, spilling into the vast expanse of life's experiences, shaping us into who we are and who we aspire to be.

The early chapters of this journey are often set in the vibrant halls of schools, where young minds first encounter the wonders of knowledge. Here, amid the echoes of reciting alphabets and the screeching of chalk on blackboards, the foundation of learning is laid. Children, wide-eyed and curious, embark on their educational odyssey, absorbing information as sponges take in water. They learn not just the intricacies of language, mathematics, and science, but also the invaluable lessons of friendship, teamwork, and resilience. These years, replete with triumphs and trials, are the building blocks of a lifelong educational structure.

As the journey progresses, the scenery changes. The structured walls of schools give way to the grand halls of universities or the challenging environments of apprenticeships and vocational training. This phase, marked by deeper exploration and specialization, is where passions are pursued and dreams start to take a definitive shape. Students delve into the realms of philosophy, engineering, arts, or whatever path they choose, each discipline offering a unique lens through which to view the world. It's a time of profound personal growth, where the seeds of ambition are nurtured by the waters of knowledge and hard work.

However, to confine education to these formal settings is to view just a fraction of its landscape. Education, in its truest form, extends far beyond. It finds its way into our homes, our workplaces, and our communities. It's present in the quiet moments we spend reading a book, in the heated debates with friends over current affairs, and in the silent observations of nature's marvels. It is in the mother teaching her child to cook, in the wisdom imparted by elders, and in the innovative ideas exchanged among colleagues.

This journey is also one of introspection and self-education. Life's trials and tribulations teach us resilience, empathy, and patience. Failures become more than mere setbacks; they transform into valuable lessons that textbooks cannot impart. Successes, on the other hand, teach us about humility and gratitude. The journey of education is thus not just about accumulating knowledge, but also about developing character and ethics. It molds us into responsible citizens, thoughtful individuals, and compassionate human beings.

Technology, in the modern era, has added exciting new dimensions to this journey. The internet, a vast ocean of information, has made learning accessible to anyone with a connection. Online courses, educational apps, and virtual classrooms have democratized education, breaking down geographical and socio-economic barriers. This digital revolution has turned the world into a giant classroom, where learning is just a click away. It encourages a culture of continuous learning, where one can pursue new skills or interests at any stage of life.

The beauty of this journey lies in its endlessness and its ability to adapt to the needs and rhythms of each individual. For some, it may involve traveling to distant lands, learning from different cultures, and gaining a global perspective. For others, it may mean staying rooted in their local communities, mastering the art of a traditional craft, or contributing to local development. Education, in this sense, is deeply personal yet universally relevant.

As we advance in age, education takes on new forms. It becomes about passing on knowledge to younger generations, about engaging in lifelong hobbies, and about learning for the sheer joy of learning. The elderly, with their treasure trove of experiences, continue to learn from the changing world around them while imparting lessons that only a life well-lived can teach.

Education is not a destination but a journey without end. It is a continuous process of growth, discovery, and enlightenment. It shapes our identity, influences our perspective, and defines our place in the world. The pursuit of knowledge, skills, and wisdom is what makes this journey a truly enriching experience, one that accompanies us from the cradle to the twilight of our lives. As we tread this path, we realize that every day is an opportunity to learn something new, to become a better version of ourselves, and to contribute positively to the world. In this grand adventure, the whole world is our classroom, and life itself is our greatest teacher.

CHAPTER 20
RELATIONSHIPS: THE TIES THAT BIND

The Psychological Perspective

Psychologically, relationships are mirrors reflecting our deepest needs, fears, and aspirations. Attachment theory, pioneered by John Bowlby, underscores the significance of early relationships in shaping our attachment styles—secure, anxious, or avoidant—which influence our adult relationships. Secure attachments foster a sense of safety and trust, whereas anxious and avoidant attachments can lead to patterns of dependency or emotional distancing.

Moreover, social identity theory posits that relationships contribute to our sense of self. Through interactions with family, friends, and even adversaries, we construct and reconstruct our identities. These relationships act as prisms, through which we view and interpret our self-image and role in the broader social fabric.

The Sociological Dimension

Sociologically, relationships form the backbone of social structures. They are the channels through which cultural norms, values, and traditions are transmitted across generations. The family unit, friendships, professional networks, and community ties each play a distinct role in maintaining the social order and facilitating societal progression.

The concept of social capital, introduced by Pierre Bourdieu, highlights how relationships can be resources. Networks of connections provide access to information, support, and opportunities, thereby influencing social mobility and the distribution of power within societies.

Emotional Landscapes

Emotionally, relationships are the crucibles within which the most intense human emotions are experienced and expressed. Love, joy, anger, jealousy, compassion, and grief are all deeply intertwined with our interactions with others. The emotional bonds we form can be sources of great joy and fulfillment, as well as pain and sorrow.

The dynamics of emotional exchange in relationships are complex. The concept of emotional intelligence, as popularized by Daniel Goleman, emphasizes the ability to recognize, understand, and manage our own emotions and those of others. This emotional acuity is crucial in navigating the ebb and flow of relational dynamics.

Communication: The Lifeline of Relationships

Effective communication is the lifeline of healthy relationships. It involves not only the exchange of words but also the non-verbal cues and emotional undertones that accompany them. Active listening, empathy, and openness are key components of constructive communication, fostering understanding and trust.

In the digital age, the modes of communication have expanded, introducing new dimensions to relationship dynamics. Social media and instant messaging, while enhancing connectivity, also present challenges such as the dilution of personal interactions and the potential for miscommunication.

Conflict and Resolution

Conflict is an inevitable aspect of relationships, arising from differences in opinions, desires, or values. However, it is not the presence of conflict, but how it is managed, that defines the health of a relationship. Effective conflict resolution involves recognizing each other's perspectives, finding common ground, and working collaboratively towards a solution.

The Evolution of Relationships

Relationships are not static; they evolve over time. Life transitions such as moving to a new city, starting a new job, or entering parenthood can significantly alter relational dynamics. Adaptability and resilience are essential in navigating these changes and sustaining the bond.

The Impact of Culture and Society

Cultural and societal contexts play a significant role in shaping relationships. Cultural norms dictate acceptable forms of relationships, roles within them, and the expression of emotions. Societal changes, such as shifting views on marriage, gender roles, and sexuality, continually redefine the landscape of personal and social relationships.

CHAPTER 21
TIME MANAGEMENT: MAKING EVERY MOMENT COUNT

In the relentless pursuit of success and fulfillment, time management stands as a pivotal skill, an indispensable tool in the arsenal of the modern professional. It's not merely about managing hours; it's about optimizing life. This chapter delves into the essence of time management, exploring strategies to make every moment count.

Understanding Time Management

Time management is the process of organizing and planning how to divide your time between specific activities. Good time management enables an individual to complete more in a shorter period, lowers stress, and leads to career success. It's about understanding the value of time, making the most of it, and ensuring that activities align with personal and professional goals.

The Illusion of Time Abundance

One of the most significant challenges in time management is the illusion that there is plenty of time. This misconception leads to procrastination and inefficient use of time. The truth is, time is a finite resource that, once lost, can never be regained. Recognizing this fact is the first step towards effective time management.

Setting Clear Goals

Time management begins with goal setting. Without a clear understanding of what you want to achieve, it becomes challenging to manage your time effectively. Goals should be SMART: Specific, Measurable, Achievable, Relevant, and Time-bound. This framework provides a clear roadmap, facilitating focused and efficient use of time.

Prioritization: The Art of Choosing

Effective time management hinges on prioritization. Not all tasks are created equal; some are more important or urgent than others. The Eisenhower Matrix, a tool for decision-making and prioritization, categorizes tasks into four quadrants: urgent and important, important but not urgent, urgent but not important, and neither urgent nor important. Focusing on tasks in the first two quadrants improves efficiency and productivity.

Time Blocking: Structuring Your Day

Time blocking is a method of time management that involves dedicating specific blocks of time to certain tasks or activities. This technique helps in maintaining focus and reducing the time lost to context switching. By allocating time blocks to tasks based on their priority, individuals can ensure a balanced approach to work and personal life.

The Role of Technology in Time Management

In today's digital era, technology plays a crucial role in time management. Various tools and apps help in scheduling, setting reminders, and tracking time spent on tasks. However, it's essential to use technology judiciously to prevent it from becoming a distraction.

Avoiding Time Wasters

Identifying and avoiding time-wasters is crucial in time management. Common time-wasters include unnecessary meetings, social media, and multitasking, which often leads to reduced efficiency and increased errors. Being aware of these pitfalls and actively working to avoid them can significantly improve time management skills.

The Importance of Breaks

Effective time management is not about working incessantly. Breaks are essential as they help in maintaining a high level of productivity throughout the day. Techniques like the Pomodoro Technique, which involves working for a set period (typically 25 minutes) followed by a short break, can enhance focus and efficiency.

Delegation: A Key to Time Management

Delegation is an often-overlooked aspect of time management. Not every task needs your personal attention. Understanding what can be delegated and to whom can free up a significant amount of time that can be better used on tasks that require your unique skills and abilities.

Continuous Improvement

The final aspect of time management is the commitment to continuous improvement. Regularly reviewing and reflecting on how you manage your time can reveal insights into what works and what doesn't, allowing for adjustments and improvements.

Making every moment count in today's fast-paced world is a challenge that demands a strategic approach to time management. By setting clear goals, prioritizing tasks, effectively using technology, and regularly reviewing practices, individuals can maximize their productivity and achieve a better work-life balance. Time management is not just a skill but a lifestyle choice that paves the way for personal and professional success.

CHAPTER 22
THE PURSUIT OF HAPPINESS: AN ETERNAL QUEST

Happiness, a term often used interchangeably with contentment, joy, and fulfillment, has been a central pursuit in human history. This eternal quest transcends cultures, geographies, and time periods, making it a universal objective of human existence. Philosophers, poets, scientists, and theologians have all grappled with the concept, attempting to define and understand the essence of true happiness.

Psychological Perspectives

From a psychological standpoint, happiness is often viewed as a state of well-being and contentment. It's a complex blend of emotions, encompassing everything from the transient joy of a pleasant experience to the deeper, enduring satisfaction with life as a whole. Positive psychology, a branch of psychology that focuses on enhancing human strengths and virtues, emphasizes the role of positive emotions, engagement, relationships, meaning, and accomplishment in cultivating happiness. This approach underscores the active pursuit of happiness, suggesting that it's not merely the absence of suffering, but the presence of positive attributes.

Philosophical Insights

Philosophically, the pursuit of happiness has been a subject of contemplation since ancient times. Greek philosophers like Aristotle viewed happiness as the highest good, achievable through the practice of virtue and reasoned living. In Eastern philosophies, such as Buddhism, happiness is often linked to the idea of detachment and the overcoming of desire, a stark contrast to the Western emphasis on the fulfillment of desires as a source of happiness. This duality presents happiness both as a result of external achievements and as an internal state of being, unaffected by the external world.

Societal and Cultural Influences

The perception of happiness is significantly shaped by cultural and societal norms. What constitutes happiness in one culture may be vastly different in another. In some societies, happiness is closely linked with material success and individual achievement, while in others, it's more about community, connection, and harmony with nature. This cultural diversity in the understanding of happiness shows that it's not a one-size-fits-all concept but a multifaceted experience influenced by a myriad of factors.

The Role of Relationships and Community

Human relationships and a sense of belonging play a crucial role in the pursuit of happiness. Studies have consistently shown that strong social connections and supportive relationships are key determinants of happiness. This highlights the importance of community, family, friendship, and love in providing a sense of security, belonging, and joy.

Challenges and Overcoming Obstacles

The pursuit of happiness is not without its challenges. Life's inherent unpredictability means that the journey towards happiness often involves navigating through hardships, losses, and disappointments. Resilience, the ability to bounce back from adversity, is a crucial skill in this pursuit. It involves not just enduring difficulties but also learning and growing from these experiences.

Practical Approaches to Happiness

Practically speaking, there are numerous strategies and habits that individuals can adopt to enhance their happiness. These include practicing gratitude, mindfulness, and kindness, pursuing goals and passions, and taking care of one's physical and mental health. The key is to find what works best for the individual, as the path to happiness is as unique as the person walking it.

Happiness, a term often used interchangeably with contentment, joy, and fulfillment, has been a central pursuit in human history. This eternal quest transcends cultures, geographies, and time periods, making it a universal objective of human existence. Philosophers, poets, scientists, and theologians have all grappled with the concept, attempting to define and understand the essence of true happiness.

Psychological Perspectives

From a psychological standpoint, happiness is often viewed as a state of well-being and contentment. It's a complex blend of emotions, encompassing everything from the transient joy of a pleasant experience to the deeper, enduring satisfaction with life as a whole. Positive psychology, a branch of psychology that focuses on enhancing human strengths and virtues, emphasizes the role of positive emotions, engagement, relationships, meaning, and accomplishment in cultivating happiness. This approach underscores the active pursuit of happiness, suggesting that it's not merely the absence of suffering, but the presence of positive attributes.

Philosophical Insights

Philosophically, the pursuit of happiness has been a subject of contemplation since ancient times. Greek philosophers like Aristotle viewed happiness as the highest good, achievable through the practice of virtue and reasoned living. In Eastern philosophies, such as Buddhism, happiness is often linked to the idea of detachment and the overcoming of desire, a stark contrast to the Western emphasis on the fulfillment of desires as a source of happiness. This duality presents happiness both as a result of external achievements and as an internal state of being, unaffected by the external world.

Societal and Cultural Influences

The perception of happiness is significantly shaped by cultural and societal norms. What constitutes happiness in one culture may be vastly different in another. In some societies, happiness is closely linked with material success and individual achievement, while in others, it's more about community, connection, and harmony with nature. This cultural diversity in the understanding of happiness shows that it's not a one-size-fits-all concept but a multifaceted experience influenced by a myriad of factors.

The Role of Relationships and Community

Human relationships and a sense of belonging play a crucial role in the pursuit of happiness. Studies have consistently shown that strong social connections and supportive relationships are key determinants of happiness. This highlights the importance of community, family, friendship, and love in providing a sense of security, belonging, and joy.

Challenges and Overcoming Obstacles

The pursuit of happiness is not without its challenges. Life's inherent unpredictability means that the journey towards happiness often involves navigating through hardships, losses, and disappointments. Resilience, the ability to bounce back from adversity, is a crucial skill in this pursuit. It involves not just enduring difficulties but also learning and growing from these experiences.

Practical Approaches to Happiness

Practically speaking, there are numerous strategies and habits that individuals can adopt to enhance their happiness. These include practicing gratitude, mindfulness, and kindness, pursuing goals and passions, and taking care of one's physical and mental health. The key is to find what works best for the individual, as the path to happiness is as unique as the person walking it.

Pursuit of happiness is an eternal quest, deeply embedded in the human experience. It is a journey that encompasses a wide range of emotions, experiences, and philosophies. While the definition of happiness may vary from person to person and culture to culture, the desire for a joyful and fulfilling life is a common thread that binds humanity. As we continue to explore and understand this complex pursuit, it remains clear that happiness, in its many forms, is an essential and enduring aspect of the human condition.

CHAPTER 23

DIGITAL DYNAMICS AND CYBER FORTRESS: MASTERING THE ART OF SECURITY IN THE DIGITAL REVOLUTION ERA

In the era of digital revolution, where technology permeates every facet of life, the importance of cyber security cannot be overstated. The digital landscape is constantly evolving, bringing new challenges and threats in the realm of cyber security. This paper delves into the critical aspects of mastering the art of security in this dynamic environment, focusing on the concept of creating a 'Cyber Fortress' to safeguard against emerging threats.

Why Cybersecurity and Personal Data Protection Matter:

- Increased Online Presence: With more activities moving online, from shopping to banking to social networking, individuals are continuously sharing

personal information. Each digital action can leave a trail of data vulnerable to theft or misuse.
- Sophistication of Cyber Threats: Cyber threats are evolving in sophistication, from phishing scams to ransomware attacks. These threats can lead to significant financial and personal losses and can affect anyone, not just large organizations.
- Impact on Privacy: There's a growing concern about how personal data is collected, used, and shared by companies. Understanding data privacy policies and the rights you have over your data is crucial.
- Regulatory Compliance: With regulations like the General Data Protection Regulation (GDPR) in Europe and various others worldwide, there is an increasing legal obligation for companies to protect personal data, impacting how they collect and handle user information.
- Empowerment Through Knowledge: Being knowledgeable about cybersecurity and data protection empowers individuals to make informed decisions about where and how they share their

information and to recognize and respond to potential threats.
- Understanding the Digital Landscape
- The Evolution of Digital Technology: The digital revolution has transformed how we interact, work, and live. With advancements in IoT, AI, and cloud computing, the complexity of digital systems has increased exponentially.
- Rising Cyber Threats: As technology advances, so do the tactics of cybercriminals. Phishing, ransomware, and DDoS attacks are becoming more sophisticated, necessitating stronger defenses.

II. The Concept of a Cyber Fortress

- Defining a Cyber Fortress: A Cyber Fortress is not just a set of tools; it's an integrated approach to digital security, combining technology, processes, and people to create a resilient defense system.
- Key Components: Essential elements include advanced firewalls, intrusion detection systems, AI-driven threat analysis, and robust encryption protocols.

III. Building the Cyber Fortress

- **Risk Assessment and Planning:** Understanding the specific threats to an organization is crucial. This involves conducting thorough risk assessments and creating strategic security plans.
- **Layered Defense Strategy:** Implementing a multi-layered security approach that includes physical, network, application, and data layers. Each layer serves as a barrier against different types of cyber attacks.
- **Continuous Monitoring and Adaptation:** Cybersecurity is not a one-time effort. Continuous monitoring and adapting to new threats are vital. This involves regular system audits, updating security protocols, and employee training.

IV. The Human Element in Cyber Security

- **Training and Awareness:** Employees are often the weakest link in cyber security. Regular training and awareness programs can significantly reduce the risk of breaches due to human error.
- **Creating a Security Culture:** Building a culture of security within the organization where every

member understands their role in maintaining cyber hygiene.

V. Advanced Technologies in Cyber Security

- Artificial Intelligence and Machine Learning: AI and ML are revolutionizing cyber security. They enable predictive analytics, anomaly detection, and automated response to threats.
- Blockchain for Enhanced Security: Blockchain technology offers a new way to secure digital transactions and data integrity.
- The Role of Quantum Computing: Exploring the potential and challenges of quantum computing in both enhancing and threatening cyber security.

VI. Dealing with Cyber Threats

- Incident Response Planning: Having a robust incident response plan is crucial. This includes procedures for threat containment, eradication, and recovery.
- Collaboration and Information Sharing: Collaborating with other organizations and sharing

information about threats can help in creating more robust security measures.
- Legal and Ethical Considerations: Understanding the legal implications of cyber attacks and the ethical considerations in cyber security practices.

VII. Future Trends and Predictions

- Emerging Threats: Discussing potential future threats, such as AI-driven attacks and deepfakes.
- Evolving Security Strategies: How cyber security strategies will need to evolve to address these emerging threats.
- The Importance of Proactive Security: Moving from a reactive to a proactive approach in cyber security.

Mastering the art of security in the digital revolution era requires a comprehensive and adaptive approach. Building a Cyber Fortress involves not just technological solutions but also a strong emphasis on the human element and continuous evolution in response to new threats. As digital dynamics continue to evolve, so must our strategies to protect against cyber threats, ensuring a secure digital future.

CHAPTER 24
NAVIGATING THE DIGITAL MAZE: THRIVING IN THE AGE OF INFORMATION OVERLOAD

In the digital era, we are inundated with a relentless stream of information. This deluge, aptly named 'information overload', presents a unique set of challenges. Understanding how to effectively navigate this digital maze is crucial for not just surviving but thriving in our hyper-connected world.

The Labyrinth of Digital Information

At first glance, the internet appears as a modern-day Library of Alexandria, a repository of human knowledge, accessible at our fingertips. However, this vast wealth of information can be as bewildering as it is empowering. Every day, we are bombarded with news articles, social media updates, emails, and advertisements, often blurring the line between essential information and digital noise. This constant stream can lead to decision fatigue, reduced attention spans, and a general sense of being overwhelmed.

The Paradox of Choice

Psychologist Barry Schwartz in his book, "The Paradox of Choice," explains how having too many options can lead to anxiety and decision paralysis. In the context of digital information, this means that the more content we have access to, the harder it becomes to choose what to focus on. This paradox is at the heart of information overload – having abundant information at our disposal, yet feeling lost in what to consume and what to ignore.

Strategies for Navigating the Maze

1. **Cultivating Digital Literacy:**

Digital literacy is no longer just about being able to use technology; it's about discerning the quality of information. It involves understanding how to locate, evaluate, and effectively use the information we find online. In an age of fake news and misinformation, being digitally literate means developing a critical eye for the source and context of the information we consume.

2. Mindful Consumption:

Mindfulness, the practice of being present and fully engaged with whatever we're doing, is a valuable tool in the fight against information overload. By being mindful of our digital consumption, we can become more selective in our focus, devoting our attention to information that is truly relevant and beneficial.

3. The Art of Unplugging:

In the relentless pursuit of staying informed, we often forget the importance of disconnecting. Regular digital detoxes, periods where we consciously step away from digital devices, can help reset our brains and reduce the stress associated with constant connectivity.

4. Leveraging Technology:

Ironically, technology itself can be a potent ally in managing information overload. Tools such as RSS feeds, content aggregators, and AI-based applications can help filter and prioritize information based on our individual preferences and needs.

5. Time Management and Setting Boundaries:

Effective time management is key. Allocating specific times for checking emails, browsing social media, and reading news can help in maintaining a balanced digital diet. Setting boundaries with technology, such as turning off notifications or having tech-free zones at home, can further aid in reducing the cognitive load.

The Role of Education and Policy

The challenge of navigating the digital maze isn't just an individual struggle; it calls for systemic changes in education and policy. Educational curriculums need to incorporate digital literacy, teaching students not just how to use technology, but how to critically assess and manage information. On a policy level, there needs to be a greater emphasis on regulating the quality of information online, ensuring that what is consumed is not just abundant but also accurate and reliable.

The Psychological Impact

The psychological impact of information overload is profound. Studies have shown that excessive digital consumption can lead to symptoms similar to attention deficit disorders, as well as increased anxiety and depression. Understanding this impact is crucial for developing personal strategies and broader societal approaches to managing information overload.

Embracing the Challenge

The digital age, with all its complexities, presents an unprecedented opportunity for growth and learning. By developing strategies to effectively navigate this digital maze, we can transform the challenge of information overload into an opportunity for personal and professional development. The key lies in understanding that in this new world, being connected doesn't just mean having access to information, but being discerning, mindful, and intentional in how we engage with the digital world. As we learn to navigate this maze, we not only survive the onslaught of information but thrive in this new era of digital enlightenment.

CHAPTER 25
COSMIC FRONTIERS: VOYAGES BEYOND EARTH'S BOUNDS

Boundless wonders and future potentials of space exploration, transcending the historical achievements to envision the path ahead. This narrative explores the uncharted realms of space, the technological innovations driving us forward, and the philosophical implications of our cosmic endeavors.

Imagining the Unseen: The Quest for the Unknown

Space, the final frontier, has always been a source of human curiosity and wonder. Unlike the historical achievements that have laid the groundwork for space exploration, the future beckons us to imagine the unseen and quest for the unknown. As we stand on the cusp of new discoveries, our understanding of the cosmos continues to evolve. The possibility of discovering new celestial bodies, understanding the mysteries of dark matter and dark energy, and even the potential of finding extraterrestrial life, are frontiers that remain tantalizingly out of reach, yet within the realm of possibility.

Technological Innovations: Paving the Way to the Stars

The journey beyond Earth's bounds is fueled by remarkable technological advancements. Future space missions may leverage propulsion systems that are currently in theoretical stages, such as antimatter engines or warp drives, promising faster interstellar travel. Moreover, advancements in artificial intelligence and robotics could lead to more sophisticated probes capable of autonomous exploration in harsh space environments. These technologies could enable us to explore not just our solar system but also the far reaches of our galaxy.

The Human Element: Adapting to the Cosmos

As we venture beyond our planet, the human element remains central. The challenges of long-duration spaceflight, including the effects on human physiology and psychology, present significant hurdles. Future explorers might rely on advanced life support systems, artificial gravity, and bioengineering to adapt to life in space. The development of space habitats, whether orbiting Earth, on the Moon, or Mars, will require us to rethink our approach to living in space, from the sustainability of resources to the social dynamics of space communities.

Astrobiology: The Search for Life Beyond Earth

One of the most compelling aspects of space exploration is the search for extraterrestrial life. The study of astrobiology, focusing on the origins and possibilities of life in the universe, drives many space missions. Future explorations may focus on the moons of Jupiter and Saturn, like Europa and Enceladus, which harbor subsurface oceans, or on exoplanets in the habitable zones of distant stars. The discovery of even microbial life beyond Earth would be a monumental achievement, profoundly altering our understanding of life in the universe.

Space as a Catalyst for Global Collaboration

Space exploration has the potential to unite humanity in a common goal. Future missions might see increased international cooperation, with countries pooling resources and expertise. This collaborative approach could lead to the establishment of international space stations, joint missions to Mars, and shared research facilities on the Moon. Space exploration could become a platform for peace, fostering a sense of shared destiny and collective stewardship of our planet.

Ethical and Philosophical Considerations

As we extend our reach into the cosmos, ethical and philosophical questions come to the forefront. The implications of terraforming planets, the potential exploitation of space resources, and the rights of future space inhabitants are complex issues that require thoughtful consideration. Moreover, the philosophical impact of discovering extraterrestrial life, or the lack thereof, could have profound implications for our understanding of our place in the universe.

Preserving Earth While Exploring Space

While we look to the stars, the importance of preserving our home planet remains paramount. Future space technologies could offer solutions to Earth's environmental challenges, from solar power satellites providing renewable energy to advancements in materials science inspired by space research. The perspective gained from space, seeing Earth as a fragile oasis, could also drive a more sustainable approach to our planet's stewardship.

A Journey Without End

A continuous quest driven by human curiosity and the desire to understand our place in the universe. As we push the boundaries of our knowledge and capabilities, we are reminded that the cosmos is not just a destination but a pathway to greater understanding and unity. Such a journey serves as a narrative of human potential and the endless possibilities that await us in the vast expanse of the universe.

COMPOSERS
FINAL THOUGHTS

Wisdom, an invaluable treasure of human experience, transcends mere knowledge or intelligence. It's a profound understanding and discernment of life, a guiding force that shapes our decisions, influences our actions, and molds our character. In a world brimming with information, yet often lacking in understanding, wisdom stands as a beacon, illuminating paths through the complexity and ambiguity of life's journey.

At its core, wisdom is the judicious application of knowledge. It's not just about accumulating facts or mastering skills, but about understanding the deeper implications of our knowledge and experiences. Wisdom involves seeing beyond the surface, recognizing patterns and connections that are not immediately apparent. It's about having the insight to discern the essence of things, to see the heart of matters.

One of the most significant aspects of wisdom is its role in decision-making. Wisdom empowers us to make choices that are not only beneficial in the short term but are also sustainable and beneficial in the long run. It helps us weigh the consequences of our actions, considering not just our own needs and desires, but also the impact on others and on the broader context of our lives.

Moreover, wisdom is inherently moral. It involves a deep understanding of right and wrong, and a commitment to live by principles that uphold the greater good. Wisdom is not self-serving; rather, it seeks to balance personal interests with the needs and well-being of others. This moral aspect of wisdom is particularly crucial in today's world, where ethical dilemmas and moral ambiguities are commonplace.

Another key aspect of wisdom is its relationship with humility. True wisdom acknowledges its own limits. It understands that there is always more to learn, more perspectives to consider, and more to understand. This humility prevents arrogance and keeps the wise open to new ideas and different viewpoints, fostering a lifelong journey of learning and growth.

Wisdom also involves emotional intelligence. It's not just about intellectual understanding but also about being attuned to emotions - both our own and those of others. Wisdom guides us in managing our emotions, helping us respond to situations with patience, empathy, and compassion. It enables us to build strong, meaningful relationships and to navigate the complexities of human interactions with grace and understanding.

In our rapidly changing world, where the only constant is change itself, wisdom provides a stable foundation. It helps us adapt, learning from the past while embracing the future. Wisdom teaches us to be resilient, to find opportunities in challenges, and to maintain hope and optimism in the face of adversity.

The pursuit of wisdom is, in many ways, the pursuit of a meaningful life. It's about seeking a deeper understanding of ourselves, our world, and our place in it. It's about striving to live a life that is not just successful in the conventional sense, but also rich in purpose and fulfillment.

Made in the USA
Columbia, SC
27 January 2024